Somebody Pray for Me

How to Pray for Your Pastor

By

Bob Piccola

XULON PRESS

Xulon Press
2301 Lucien Way #415
Maitland, FL 32751
407.339.4217
www.xulonpress.com

© 2020 by Bob Piccola

All rights reserved solely by the author. The author guarantees all contents are original and do not infringe upon the legal rights of any other person or work. No part of this book may be reproduced in any form without the permission of the author. The views expressed in this book are not necessarily those of the publisher.

Unless otherwise indicated, Scripture quotations are from *The Holy Bible*, New American Standard Version (NASB). Other versions will be notated by an abbreviation. For example: Bible in Basic English (BBE) New Living Translation (NLT) New International Version (NIV) New King James Version (NKJV)

Printed in the United States of America.

ISBN-13: 978-1-6312-9372-6

Dedication

This book is dedicated to congregation members who desire to support and pray for their leaders in a deeper way. It is also dedicated to pastors and leaders who long for their followers to run with the vision that they impart to them regularly. I want to give a special shout out to my wife, Connie, with whom I have been married thirty-eight years. Her prayers and support through the years have had a profound effect on our ministry together.

Foreword

This book should be mandatory for every believer. The calling of the pastor is a gift, but the gift is not for the pastor. The calling of the pastor is a gift to the church. Ephesians 4:8 says, "Therefore it says, 'When He ascended on high, He led captive a host of captives, and He gave gifts to men.'" This statement is followed by verse eleven which states, "So Christ Himself gave the apostles, the prophets, the evangelists, the pastors and teachers, to equip his people for works of service, so that the body of Christ may be built up" (NIV). When you receive a gift, there are usually instructions on the proper use and care of that gift. This book is a good manual for the proper care of your pastor. Hebrews 13:17-18a says, "Have confidence in your leaders and submit to their authority, because they keep watch over you as those who must give an account. Do this so that their work will be a joy, not a burden, for that would be of no benefit to you. Pray for us" (NIV).

I believe many of the ministers who have fallen by the wayside have done so because there was not enough prayer for them. When the Israelites were in a battle and Moses was holding up his arms the Israelites were winning, but then when he got tired and his arms dropped, they began to lose. Aaron and Hur came along and held up his arms, and there was total victory. When people hold up the pastor in prayer, there is total victory for everyone.

Rev. Sylvia Miley, Cofounder of Faith Covenant Ministries

Table of Contents

Dedication v
Foreword vii
Intro xi

1. Can I Get Some Prayer? Please? 1
2. Rapid Growth 7
3. Protection 13
4. A Fearless Word 23
5. Open Doors 29
6. Clarity 33
7. Integrity 37
8. Praying the Word 45
9. Let's Start Praying 55

Intro

It is easy for us to see when people need prayer. Right? We usually pray for those who are the weakest among us. Maybe someone you know is going through a tough time in their life or in their walk with God. From our vantage point, it seems like they make mistake after mistake. In fact, I am sure you know some folks that could not make a right decision if their life depended on it, and often it does. Some people just have a knack for being wrong. Sometimes, it is like Jamie Reagan said on the television series Blue Bloods, "It seems like God has it in for some people and all you can do is stand five hundred feet back and watch." Now, we know that God does not have it in for us, but it may seem like that to us sometimes. Some people develop a habit of making wrong choices, bad relationships, or financial miss-steps that have made it almost impossible for them to get past and into their destiny in God. All of us may have said at one time or another, something along the lines of, "So-and-so is really going to need a lot of prayer." Or "They really need a touch from God." How about the old standard, "Bless their heart"? What I would like you to see is that there are always two sides to the coin. Let me explain.

On the one side, we need to notice those that are in need and be ready to minister to them. In fact, the Bible says in James 1:27, "Religion that God our Father accepts as pure and faultless is this: to look after orphans and widows in their distress and to keep oneself from being polluted by the world" (NIV). Although this is talking about providing for their physical needs, it also speaks about taking care of their spirits, and that means by prayer. The apostle James is telling us to make sure we meet the needs of the neediest among us, both physically and spiritually.

On the other side of the coin, those that God has put in leadership over us need our prayers just as much. Contrary to what some might think, pastors, and all spiritual leaders for that matter, need the prayers of the saints just as much. When I was the senior pastor of a thriving church, I coveted the prayers of my congregation. In fact, I still have people who have committed to pray for me regularly. All leaders need our prayers. Apostles, prophets, evangelists, pastors, teachers, worship leaders, children's church teachers, youth leaders, you get the picture. We as leaders need the prayers of our flock and we are comforted to know that they are praying for us. Leaders need prayer not because they are weak, but because they are strong and need to remain strong, so strength can be imparted through them.

Pastors need the saints' prayers because as leaders they are at the forefront of the attacks of the enemy. They continuously live on the front lines of spiritual battle. All leaders live with a bull's eye on their backs. The attacks against them are relentless. I am not trying to paint a bleak picture of leadership, but it's true that leaders have a lot of opposition to handle. We are called by God to the ministry. It's our life and we love it. We do it because we love the Lord and we love His people. The simple fact is that most of the time, people do not know what we are going through. But we go through stuff just like you. We look strong, and we are. We don't complain, and we shouldn't, because we are the leader. What kind of respect would you have for a pastor that constantly complained about his or her problems? But we live in the same world that you live in and experience most everything you do. Jesus Himself said in John 16:33, "These things I have spoken to you, so that in Me you may have peace. In the world you have tribulation but take courage; I have overcome the world." Jesus made us a promise. Jesus gave us lots of promises that I love and receive, but this one I wish He had not. He promised that we would all have tribulations. That is not just talking about the average church person. That includes leaders, ministers, even the greatest of preachers and leaders throughout the centuries. We all have one thing in common – TROUBLES. Along with the bull's eye on our backs, you can see tire tracks across our chest from the times we have been thrown under the bus. Most leaders hide their bumps, bruises, and scars well, but you can be sure we have them. The world is more than happy to run over your leaders any chance it gets. This we should know for sure:

YOUR PASTORS ARE STRONG, AND THEY STILL NEED YOUR PRAYERS!

The apostle Paul coveted the prayers of his followers. There are several instances in scripture where he said, "Pray for me" or "Pray that I..." We are going to study those scriptures and find out just how Paul instructed his followers to pray for him. By the time we are done, you will know exactly what to pray and how to pray it. You will also see that when we pray for certain things for our pastors, we will also be praying similar thing for ourselves. It is like a two-edged sword and a double blessing. Wouldn't you like that blessing along with your pastor?

Chapter One

CAN I GET SOME PRAYER? PLEASE?

1 Timothy 2:1
"First of all, then, I urge that entreaties and prayers, petitions and thanksgivings, be made on behalf of all men."

There are many ways that you can show your pastor that you stand with him/her and support the vision of the church. Some of those ways are showing up at church, taking your place as a volunteer, tithing, and giving offerings, and echoing the vision of the church to others. But I would have to say that one of the greatest ways we support our leaders is by praying for them. When we pray for our leaders, we engage with them on a deeper level. We bring Holy Spirit into our relationship with them. That relationship becomes more than just them being your pastor and you sitting there looking up at them every Sunday. Whenever we pray for somebody, anybody, it takes us to a deeper level with them and we begin to see them as God does.

There are many passages in the Bible about learning to pray, examples of people praying, and leaders asking for prayer. The person who stands out the most to me is the apostle Paul. Many times, Paul would say things like pray for me, pray for us, or just simply pray. He knew that he needed the prayers of his followers and he was not afraid to ask for them. My good friend Gary Hines often says, "Pray for me because I need the prayer and you need the practice." But Paul did not ask for prayer because he was complaining. He did not ask for prayer because he was hurt or abused or persecuted, even though he was. He asked for prayer because he knew that he needed the power of God in his life and he knew that the best way to get that power was to ask his followers to pray for him.

If your leader is worth their salt, they will not complain to you. They will probably never share their personal issues with you. You may never know what they are going through or even if they are going through something. It is not because they do not love you. It is the exact opposite; they do love you and they want to be an example of faith and strength. They are people of character, integrity, and faith. You would probably not be following them if they were not people of...

- Faith
- Vision
- Character
- Wisdom
- Great love–for God and for you

Those characteristics are what drive leaders to be examples. Paul said in 1 Corinthians 11:1, "Be imitators of me, just as I also am of Christ." You would not want to imitate someone that complained constantly or was in fear all the time. Would you?

The phrase "be imitators" is one word in the Greek language. It is the word *mimētēs*[1] and it means to be a follower. It carries with it the idea of mimicking the teacher. Not just doing what they tell you to do but doing what they do. That is an awesome responsibility that every leader should take seriously. And Paul did. That is why he asked his followers to pray for him. Paul asked for very specific prayers five different times, and then the writer of Hebrews asks for prayer as well. Now, the reason I distinguish between Paul and the writer of Hebrews is because it is unclear as to the authorship of the book of Hebrews. Some scholars believe it was Paul. It could be that his apostolic team all had input. We just don't know. Whether it is or isn't is an argument for another day. We will focus on the actual prayer request in the case of Hebrews. The five requests from Paul and the one from the book of Hebrews form the basis of the teaching in this book, and we'll explore each prayer request in depth with the goal of learning how to pray Bible-based prayers for our pastors and leaders.

The word of God is the basis for all our prayers. There are those times when we do not know what to pray and we cry out with the most famous two-word prayer, "JESUS HELP"! There are also times when we do not know what to pray and Holy Spirit helps us. Romans 8: 26-27 says, "In the same way the Spirit also helps our weakness; for we do not know how to pray as we should, but the Spirit Himself intercedes for us with groanings too deep for words; and He who searches the hearts knows what the mind of the Spirit is, because He intercedes for the saints according to the will of God." These are the times when we pray in the Spirit for our leaders. But the word of God is also clear on what we ought to pray as per Paul's requests. This is called praying the will of God and it is the most effective and powerful way we can pray. When we know the will of God and we speak it, we move from fear-based praying to faith-based praying. Remember, we are seated with Christ in heavenly places. Ephesians 2:6 says that He "raised us up with Him and seated us with Him in the heavenly places in Christ Jesus." This is a place of governing authority and we exercise that governance by speaking and praying the will and the word of God.

We should look at one more verse concerning praying the will of God. 1 John 5:14-15 says, "This is the confidence which we have before Him, that, if we ask anything according to His will, He hears us. And if we know that He hears us in whatever we ask, we know that we have the requests which we have asked from Him." Don't you want that confidence to know that your prayers are being answered? This holds true not only with prayers for leaders, but anything we pray for. John is saying that if we ask for anything according to the will of God, we can have confidence in the fact that He hears us, and if we know He hears us, we can know that He will answer us. Wow! That is a powerful promise. Know the will of God in His word. Pray it. God will answer His own will. Jeremiah 1:12 says, "Then the Lord said to me, 'You have seen well, *for I am watching over My word to perform it*'" (emphasis mine). He watches over His word, not our words.

Now, we know that there is often much opposition and difficulty inside the church and outside the church. Pastors and leaders constantly need the people of God to pray for them. The shepherd needs the prayers of the sheep as much as the sheep need the prayers of the shepherd. Don't forget, your leader is also one of Christ's sheep and can be susceptible to the same problems, issues, and circumstances as you. As a leader, they ought to be mature enough to withstand the temptations and weaknesses, but our prayers are so important to their strength and success. There are many things we could do for them. Many prayers we could pray on our own. Sometimes we're afraid to ask what we can pray for. You might say, "I don't know what to pray." They never complain, they never ask, they only give. As I said before, the best thing that we can pray for our leaders or anybody else for that matter, is the word of God. That's right. The Bible is full of leaders asking their people to pray specific prayers for them. The apostle Paul was not afraid to ask his people to pray for him. His prayer requests were specific and to the point.

One thing I want to say before we go on is that when we pray for people, we don't *pray over* them. Especially leaders. The Bible says that they are over us. This is not a lording or ruling position but rather a place of responsibility for us as sheep. Hebrews 13:17 says, "Obey your leaders and submit to them, for they keep watch over your souls as those who will give an account. Let them do this with joy and not with grief, for this would be unprofitable for you." Obey and submit because they must give an account for you, and it would be unprofitable for you if they had to give a bad report. Don't give your leaders grief! Pray for them. 1 Timothy 2:1-3 says, "First of all, then, I urge that entreaties and prayers, petitions and thanksgivings, be made on behalf of all men, for kings and all who are in authority, so that we may lead a tranquil and quiet life in all godliness and dignity. This is good and acceptable in the sight of God our Savior." This scripture carries with it an attitude of humility and thankfulness for leaders. It does not give any idea of manipulation or *praying over* them.

The term *pray over* is a very popular term these days. It is used often in intercessory circles, prophetic and apostolic circles and has a lot to do with making declarations and proclamations. While I agree very strongly with the concept of declaring and decreeing, and I practice it daily, we need to be careful that we are not manipulating others with our prayers. We must never pray our own will for them. We never pray "change" over our leaders. It is not our job to change them. It's God's. We must make sure when we pray, that we are praying the will of God for the leader, person, or even region. 1 Thessalonians 5:12-13 says, "But we request of you, brethren, that you appreciate those who diligently labor among you, and have charge over you in the Lord and give you instruction, and that you esteem them very highly in love because of their work. Live in peace with one another."

As we pray for our leaders, there should always be a sense of honor, respect, and appreciation for them. Never manipulation or forcing your own will on them. We should never have the idea that we are praying for a pastor because we have the word of the Lord and they don't. I cannot count how many times people have come to me with a "word from the Lord" and when I heard it, I thought, where in the world did that come from? This is how the apostle Peter addresses this subject in 2 Peter 1:20-21, "But know this first of all, that no prophecy of Scripture is a matter of one's own interpretation, for no prophecy was ever made by an act of human will, but men moved by the Holy Spirit spoke from God." So you see, even when we pray the word of God or have a prophetic word for the pastor, it should never be with the idea that I am an agent of change and I'm bringing a word of correction to this pastor. Your pastor or leader should be in relationship with a peer or a ministry father that can speak into his or her life. That relationship is formed by years of trust and service. It is never taken lightly or irreverently but with the fear of the Lord speaking the truth in love. It is not the sheep's job to bring correction to the shepherd.

That is not to say that people shouldn't have a word for their pastor, but it should never be a correctional or directional word. It should be a word of support and confirmation to the vision that the leader has already cast to the people. I will never forget what Pastor Bob Yandian said about people who had the word of the Lord for him. He said very plainly, "You are not Holy Spirit for me."

So, how can we pray for our pastors and leaders? We pray the word of God from the Bible. When you do not know what to pray, even when you think you do know what to pray, pray the word. There are six very appropriate and powerful scriptures that we can pray. The following chapters will be a study of the prayers the apostle Paul asked for; these are prayers that all of us in leadership desire.

Chapter Two

RAPID GROWTH

2 Thessalonians 3:1
"Finally, brethren, pray for us that the word of the Lord will spread rapidly and be glorified, just as it did also with you."

Prayer is one of the fundamental practices of every Christian. It ranks right up there with reading your Bible, witnessing, tithing, going to church, and having a lifestyle of worship. In fact, prayer and worship are two sides of the same coin. Jesus taught about this in Matthew 21:13. He said to them, "It is written, 'My house shall be called a house of *prayer,*' but you are making it a robber's den" (emphasis mine). The word translated as prayer in the original language is *proseuchē*.[2] It means prayer, but it also means worship. I think it is interesting that we try to separate prayer and worship as being two different acts but they both come from the same word. My father in the faith Dr. James Miley always said that worship is the highest form of prayer because it focuses on God Himself and not just the need that we are praying for. Prayer is just another form of worship.

We come to our first example of the apostle Paul asking for prayer for himself. It may not be the first chronologically, but it is first on my list and that's what's really import. Just kidding. Let us look at the verse. 2 Thessalonians 3:1, "Finally, brethren, pray for us that the word of the Lord will spread rapidly and be glorified, just as it did also with you." There are really two requests here. The first request is that the word of the Lord would spread rapidly. The second is that the word of the Lord would be glorified. These are both very important needs of a pastor.

Let us look at the first. Paul asked the Thessalonians to pray that the word of the Lord would spread rapidly. What is the *word* of the Lord? That can mean many things depending on who is delivering it and who is hearing it. That verse uses the Greek word *logos*.[3] This has many meanings. We understand that Jesus Himself is the logos. The gospel of John starts out with this declaration in John 1:1, "In the beginning was the Word, and the Word was with God, and the Word was God." *Word* is used three times here talking about Jesus Himself. He is the revealed word of God. The logos.

In this case however, Paul is talking about the word that he preaches. Which is also the logos. Of course, the word he preached is Jesus, and Him crucified, as he declared in 1 Corinthians 2:2, "For I determined to know nothing among you except Jesus Christ, and Him crucified." But that word is also the vision that Paul casts for the churches for whom he is the apostle. I believe this relates very well to the vision that your pastor casts for your church. We don't need to get into a discussion about whether the senior team leader is an apostle, prophet, evangelist, pastor or teacher. One of the senior leader's primary responsibility is to cast vision for the organization or the team. It is your primary job to run with that vision. Habakkuk 2:2 says, "Then the Lord answered me and said, 'Record the vision and inscribe it on tablets, that the one who reads it may run.'" Somebody must cast the vision, and somebody must run with it.

Can I ask you a pretty direct question? Do you know what the vision for your church is? Your pastor does. Chances are, he/she is trying to teach you that vision. It is the word of the Lord to your community. If I might speak about myself for a minute, I try to include some aspect of the vision of my church in every message I preach. I also have specific times throughout the year that I call Vision Sunday. Last January, we launched A Month of Vision where I spent four weeks just talking about the vision of our church. There are many messages that God speaks to us through His word. The vision of your church is one of those messages. Take the time to know and understand what the vision of your church is. Take part in communicating it alongside your pastor. If you want your church to grow, echo the vision your pastor preaches to others. If you want to get close to your pastor, echo the vision. If you want to be in leadership, you guessed it, echo the vision. It will change your life and bring life to your local church community.

Pray that the vision spreads and that it *spreads rapidly*. The word *spread* is *trechō*[4] which means to run or walk hastily. Spreading is an action word. It means something is happening. It is growing. It is getting into people and places that it hasn't been before. The word is moving forward at a quick pace. When was the last time you have seen some forward motion in your church? Pray that the message and the vision spreads throughout your community.

If the word is spreading, that means that someone like you who runs with the vison is spreading it to others who hear and then respond to it. It means your church is going to grow and new people are coming in to run with the vision just like you are. That is making disciples, isn't it? Rapid growth means your church is going to grow fast. Wouldn't that be awesome? Maybe you have noticed that your church has not grown in a while. When was the last time a first-time visitor showed up? Instead of complaining about it, why don't you pray that the vision would spread rapidly? That is a novel idea. Praying instead of complaining.

When you pray that the vision spreads, you are praying a two-edged sword. You are also praying for yourself that the word would spread rapidly inside of you. Your community gets the prayer, and you get the prayer. You pray for them and yourself at the same time. Now here is a key, if you are praying for the word to spread rapidly, then you better get that word into yourself in a hurry. Because people are going to start coming, and guess who is going to have to help your pastor share the vision with them? You guessed it. You are. Now here is something I really need you to understand. If you are praying that the word spreads rapidly, and you are hearing the word, then you should not complain about what is being said. You must get in step with what your pastor is preaching our else your prayers are in vain. You must receive the word just like everyone else. Did you ever notice that some folks seem to feel like they are above what is being preached? They sit there with their arms folded and shake their heads up and down occasionally, but they really don't receive it. We cannot be like that. We must receive the word like he is preaching just to us.

We need to pray that the message spreads. Jesus said in Matthew 11:12, "And from the days of John the Baptist till now, the kingdom of heaven is forcing its way in, and men of force take it" (BBE). I love that wording, *forcing its way in*. This is a violent, aggressive spreading of the message. Sounds pretty rapid to me. It is all about God's kingdom growing, which is the essence of the Great Commission. Matthew 28:19-20 says, "Go therefore and make disciples of all the nations, baptizing them in the name of the Father and the Son and the Holy Spirit, teaching them to observe all that I commanded you; and lo, I am with you always, even to the end of the age."

Remember, it is the great commission not the great suggestion. A commission is much more powerful than a suggestion. When someone *commissions*[5] you to do something, they are giving you authority to do certain functions. When we pray the word of God for somebody, we act in the authority that the word carries with it. Whether it is a Bible verse or the vision of your church. It really doesn't matter. Pray the word of God for your pastor. Pray that the word spreads rapidly.

But that verse in 2 Thessalonians does not stop at that. There is a second part in 2 Thessalonians 3:1, "Finally, brethren, pray for us that the word of the Lord will spread rapidly *and be glorified*, just as it did also with you" (emphasis mine). When we pray that the word is glorified, it means that the vision of your church and your pastor is being honored and glorified as they should. Your community should not see your church as just another church or your pastor as just another pastor. They should see your church's vision as something special, just as you should. They will see it that way when you embrace it as something special. When it becomes a part of your life. They will see your pastor as special when you begin to treat him/her that way and when you honor them as they deserve. 1 Timothy 5:17 says, "The elders who rule well are to be considered worthy of double honor, especially those who work hard at preaching and teaching." They are not just one of the boys. They deserve honor and should be treated with the respect that is due them. How will the world honor the things of God when His people do not? Honor is a tricky thing. It is difficult for us to honor people for several reasons.

A.   Past Failures.

We've seen so many men and women of God fall in recent years. That indirectly puts a stain on all of us. The pressures of ministry and the temptations that follow those pressures can take their toll on someone who is not cared for, prayed for, and supported properly.

B.   Honoring them points out our own insecurities.

Some people feel that if they give honor to someone else, it takes something away from themselves. This couldn't be farther from the truth. Jesus said in Luke 6:38, "Give, and it will be given to you. They will pour into your lap a good measure—pressed down, shaken together, and running over. For by your standard of measure it will be measured to you in return." Now, I know we like to use this verse when we are receiving offerings, but the context of this verse is about loving your enemies and relating to others. If we give honor, we will receive honor, pressed down, shaken together, and running over. Don't limit this verse to just money. The Bible also says in 1 Thessalonians 5:12, "Dear brothers and sisters, *honor* those who are your leaders in the Lord's work. They work hard among you and give you spiritual guidance" (NLT) (emphasis mine). There is no hidden meaning in the Greek for the word *honor*. It means treat your leaders with respect and hold them in high regard.

There are many great books about how to treat your pastor. I particularly like the book written by Dr. Mark Barkley called *How to Relate to Your Pastor*. In the introduction, Dr. Barkley says, "There is no way the Bible teaches us that our pastors are to be 'just like us.' Neither does it teach that a pastor should condescend to a lower level or lifestyle in order to walk with others. Everyone from every walk of life knows that you look up to your leaders and heroes."[6]

Do you see your pastor as a hero? How about your youth pastor or worship pastor? Do not be afraid of giving honor to your leaders. It is a Biblical principle and it will draw others to the message. Pray for your leaders that the message would spread rapidly and be honored throughout the community, the region, and the world. And when they do get the honor, be proud of them and work hard at being just like them.

Chapter Three

PROTECTION

2 Thessalonians 3:2
*"And that we will be rescued from perverse and evil men;
for not all have faith."*

This request is a continuation of Paul's request in verse one to pray that the word would spread rapidly, and it is part of the same sentence. The onslaught of the enemy against your pastor can be overwhelming at times. When Paul is asking to be rescued, he is really asking for protection. Asking for protection from perverse and evil men seems like a no brainer, right? Why would we want perverse and evil people to interfere with the rapid spreading of the word of the Lord? But he is not asking for protection only from people outside the church. It is easy to see unbelievers as perverse and evil. The political arena and the entertainment industry, for example, can be hostile to church, your pastor, and Christianity in general. But by looking deeper at the words perverse and evil, we see that this is not just talking about unbelievers. This is also speaking about perverse and evil men inside the church. These are people who disrupt and cause division. This is a continuous tactic of the enemy, to destroy a church from within. Abraham Lincoln said, "America will never be destroyed from the outside. If we falter and lose our freedoms, it will be because we destroyed ourselves."[7] The attack originates from the spirit realm, but the weapon often used is people. You will see more clearly what I am saying when we take a deeper look at the words *perverse* and *evil*.

Let us look at the word *evil* first. Lots of pictures enter our minds when we hear or read the word evil. A picture paints a thousand words, but some words paint many pictures and evil is one of them. Pictures of Hitler, Stalin, and Manson to name a few. The two planes crashing into the World Trade Center buildings elicit an emotional response from every American to this day. But this word evil has a different implication. The Greek word for *wicked* [8] infers out of place, improper, injurious, amiss, harmful, and unreasonable. Maybe you have run into some of these people in church.

A. People who always wants to argue.

Some people are always ready for a fight. You say one thing, they say the opposite, not necessarily because they believe it, but in order to stir up trouble. They live for it. They thrive on controversy and then they walk away leaving a mess for the pastor to clean up. There is almost nothing more frustrating to a preacher than someone challenging him/her, especially in a meeting. It is not the actual disagreement that frustrates the pastor, but the fact that some folk think they always know better than the pastor. They heard somebody say something else or they saw a video on You-tube. Or the all-time great argument, "It's not our tradition". They never consider whether the preacher studied for hours for that message or that God spoke something to him to give to the congregation. Proverbs 20:3 says, "Keeping away from strife is an honor for a man, but any fool will quarrel." The Bible calls a quarrelsome person a fool. It also says that a person who stays away from arguing deserves honor. Pray for protection against people like this for your pastor, and don't be one of those quarrelsome people yourself.

B. People who say, "It can't be done"

This is a destructive attitude which strikes out against the very vision the Lord has given a church. People who say this are living by what they see and not by faith. 2 Corinthians 5:7 says, "For we walk by faith, not by sight." We need to pray that our leaders are surrounded by people who are faith people and not sight people. Faithless people will suck the life out of any leader and any ministry. They judge every situation by what they see and not by what the word of God says. Isn't that what Jesus accused the Pharisees of doing in John 8:15a, when He told them, "You judge according to the flesh." Leaders need people around them that will be full of faith and judge by the Spirit. The apostle Paul said a lot about this in Romans 8:5-8, "For those who are according to the flesh set their minds on the things of the flesh, but those who are according to the Spirit, the things of the Spirit. For the mind set on the flesh is death, but the mind set on the Spirit is life and peace, because the mind set on the flesh is hostile toward God; for it does not subject itself to the law of God, for it is not even able to do so, and those who are in the flesh cannot please God." In Numbers chapter 13, Moses sent twelve spies into Canaan to scope out the land. When they came back, ten of the spies were filled with fear and told Moses they could not take the land. This caused great fear among the people. One man, Caleb, filled with faith, quieted the people down and gave the encouraging word that they indeed could take the land and that they should. This is the kind of person every pastor needs to surround themselves with. The kind of person that says what Jesus said in the second part of Matthew 19:26, "With people this is impossible, but with God all things are possible." Now when you pray like this, you are also praying for yourself. If you are one of the people that surround your pastor, then you need to become the very thing you are praying for, that is, a person of faith.

C. People who say, "It's never been done before"

Let's face it, most people don't like change. But sometimes change is needed to get a different result. Albert Einstein said that the definition of insanity is doing the same thing over and over expecting a different result. Resistance to change can really harm an organization. Some people just dig their feet in the ground and refuse to move. They say, "We never did it like that before," to which I would reply, "That's why they call it new." There is also the frequently used phrase, "My old church used to do it like this." Well, you're not in your old church anymore, Dorothy. Don't you remember? You left there for a reason.

The book of Genesis is the book of beginnings and a book of firsts. There are many recorded firsts in the book of Genesis. They are either the first-time certain words or concepts were introduced in the Bible, or they are first time man experienced something new about God. These words or concepts are new mostly because God was introducing Himself to man. But it also shows that He is creative and does new things. These firsts in Genesis are also interesting because the law of first mention.

> "Those who study the Bible in a serious way sometimes refer to the Law of First Mention. It is not so much a law, really, as a common principle in the Scriptures. If you select an important biblical word—say, *worship*—you will find that its first Biblical appearance sets the tone for all the richness of meaning that will emerge. Through the Word we go on to find many new understandings and many variations on the theme, but the first cut is the deepest; the First Mention gives us the essential picture."[9]

In Genesis we find the first mention of:

Blessing (Gen. 1:28)
Marriage (Gen. 2:21-24)
Lie (Gen. 3:4)
Sin (Gen. 3:6)
Divine curse (Gen. 3:14-19)
Messianic prophecy (Gen. 3:15)
Pain in childbirth (Gen. 3:16)
Labor (Gen. 3:17)
Thistles (Gen. 3:18)
Sweat (Gen. 3:19)
Clothes (Gen. 3:21)

Baby (Gen. 4:1)
Religious offering (Gen. 4:3-4)
Animal sacrifice (Gen. 4:4)
Murder (Gen. 4:8)
Death (Gen. 4:8)
Farm (Gen. 4:2)
Shepherd (Gen. 4:2)
City (Gen. 4:17)
Polygamy (Gen. 4:19)
Cattle herd (Gen. 4:20)
Music (Gen. 4:21)

Metal works (Gen. 4:22)
Boat (Gen. 6:14)
Rain (Gen. 7:12)
Altar (Gen. 8:20)
Eating of meat (Gen. 9:3)
Capital punishment (Gen. 9:6)
Covenant (Gen. 9:9)
Rainbow (Gen. 9:12-17)
Case of drunkenness (Gen. 9:21)
World unity movement (Gen. 11:4)
Languages (Gen. 11:6-9)
King (Gen. 14:1)
War (Gen. 14:1-2)
Priest (Gen. 14:18)
Tithing (Gen. 14:20)
Justification by faith (Gen. 15:6)
Animosity between the Arabs & the Jews (Gen. 16)
Meeting between angels & men (Gen. 18:1-3)
Intercessory prayer (Gen. 18:23-32)
Homosexuality (Gen. 19:4-5)
Incest (Gen. 19:30-38)
Answered prayer (Gen. 20:17)
Twins (Gen. 25:24)
Dream (Gen. 28:12)
Prison (Gen. 39:20)
Famine (Gen. 41:27)

Some of these words we use every day and really don't even think about them, but these were all new experiences for Adam and Eve, Abraham, Isaac and Jacob. Oh, and let's not forget Joseph. God loves new things. Isaiah 43:19 says, "Behold, I will do something new, Now it will spring forth; Will you not be aware of it? I will even make a roadway in the wilderness, rivers in the desert." Do not resist the new things your leaders are trying to do. Pray for them. Help them embrace the change.

D. People who try to manipulate

We have all had people in our lives that are opinionated and strong in their convictions. They know what they believe and are confident in their calling and ability to lead people. Then there are people who try to manipulate others. Manipulation is abuse. It is an extreme negotiation, control or influence to gain the advantage over someone else. It is the desire to enforce your will over another. Manipulators will do anything they can to have their way. I have seen many people try to manipulate pastors and churches to create and enforce their own vision. These things can happen especially in the apostolic, prophetic, and intercessory circles. Their favorite phrase is "The Lord told me..." It shuts down any further conversation about the matter because it implies that, since God said it, there cannot be any further discussion. Who wants to go against the word of the Lord? People need to be sure that something is a word from the Lord before they share it and not just their own desire for a thing to happen. Leaders need to be careful with this because it is their responsibility to get the word of the Lord for their congregation. No apostle, prophet or intercessor can be Holy Spirit for your pastor. However, that does not mean that we shouldn't have people that we trust to speak into our lives. But a prophetic word from the Lord should contain words of confirmation of something that is already in your leader's heart.

Manipulation finds its roots in demonic activity. The original sin took place because the serpent manipulated Eve into doubting the word of God, and she in turn manipulated her husband. Genesis 3:1 says, "Now the serpent was more crafty than any beast of the field which the Lord God had made. And he said to the woman, 'Indeed, has God said, "You shall not eat from any tree of the garden"'"? (emphasis mine). In some uses, this word *crafty* means prudent but not in this case. Strong's concordance defines this word as meaning cunning, shrewd, crafty and sly.[10] It gives the idea of a person who is ready to do anything to enforce their own will or vision. This is manipulation. When there is more than one vision, it is di-vision. One of the greatest privileges and responsibilities a pastor has is to cast the vision the Lord has given to him for the local church. That vision often comes though fasting and prayer and seeking the Lord. Many of us are familiar with the verse on vision from Habakkuk 2:2. It says, "Then the Lord answered me and said, 'Record the vision and inscribe it on tablets, that the one who reads it may run.'" It is the pastor's job to teach and convey the vision, it is the congregation's job to run with the vision. We need to pray for our leaders that they be protected from manipulation. We should also be praying that the Lord would expose this kind of behavior as demonic.

This crafty, cunning behavior is a rebellious attitude and must be dealt with as such. 1 Samuel 15:23 says, "For rebellion is as the sin of divination, and insubordination is as iniquity and idolatry. Because you have rejected the word of the Lord, He has also rejected you from being king." Rebellion is like witchcraft. This controlling, manipulating practice does not come from Holy Spirit. Samuel goes on to use the word *insubordination*[11]. This is a scary word. It means to be insolent, arrogant, and presumptuous, to press and to be stubborn. People who do anything to force their own will on a situation are manipulative, abusive, and as we just read in the scripture, are likened to those who practice witchcraft. Pray that your pastor would be protected from such people.

E. People who talk behind the pastor's back

Talking behind a person's back is gossip, plain and simple. It is another form of manipulation because it tries to get people to see things the way you see them. Gossip is never good whether it is with one another or with your leaders. The Bible is noticeably clear about gossip. Psalms 101:5 says, "Whoever secretly slanders his neighbor, him I will destroy." That is harsh language from God Himself. Gossip may seem to start innocently, but it eventually hurts and can destroy the person the gossip is about. God says He will destroy the gossiper.

Proverbs instructs us to not even associate with a gossiper. Proverbs 20:19 states, "He who goes about as a slanderer reveals secrets, therefore do not associate with a gossip." After reading this, some of us may want to reconsider some of the relationships we have and whether they are healthy enough to continue. Do not be a gossiper. Do not hang out with gossipers. Do not use prayer requests to gossip about people. Proverbs 18:21 says, "Death and life are in the power of the tongue, and those who love it will eat its fruit." What kind of fruit are you producing today? What kind of fruit are you eating today?

F. People who are always in a hurry

Just as there are people who do not like change, there are those who think that change just can't happen fast enough. They are always on the move. Ambition and discontent fill their hearts. They are opportunists that use any situation as a stepping-stone for their ministry. They may have gotten a word from the Lord, a vision from God, a dream, or a prophetic experience of some kind and they want to move on it immediately. They want it to happen right now! All throughout Christian history, there are those who have taken it upon themselves to be the ones that fulfill the will of God for their generation. Now, while it is true that this is our calling, we can't do things outside of the timing of God. This again is another form of manipulation. We manipulate our circumstances to conform to what we think we see. Notice I said *what we think we see*. I say that because many times we do not know exactly what we are seeing, nor do we have a clear and complete understanding of what the vision is yet.

God's vision, whatever it may be, will always be greater than our own understanding and abilities. And we need to wait on His timing to do it. Again, we look to the wisdom of the apostle Paul. 1 Corinthians 4:5 says, "Therefore judge nothing before the appointed time; wait until the Lord comes. He will bring to light what is hidden in darkness and will expose the motives of the heart. At that time each will receive their praise from God" (NIV). We read previously from Habakkuk 2:2 about writing the vision down and running with it. The second part of that thought is in Habakkuk 2:3, "For the vision is yet for *the appointed time*; it hastens toward the goal and it will not fail. Though it tarries, *wait for it*; for it will certainly come, it will not delay" (emphasis mine). *The appointed time; wait for it.* There is an appointed time for every vision. We must wait. Now, waiting does not mean standing around and doing nothing. It means that we are seeking the Lord about the vision. We are praying about it. We are worshiping and serving God to the best of our ability, doing what we know to do. We must work at it, but we must do things in the timing of God. Do not get ahead of God or even ahead of yourself. There is a process to the vision. Your character and integrity are vital part of that process. We may be gifted at certain things, but what allows us to sustain that gifting is our character and integrity.

Many leaders fall because of a weakness in their character. Ministers who have fallen into sinful practices due to a lack of character and integrity have brought disgrace to the name of Christ. Since Satan has ministers of the gospel (and their families) locked in his sight, and since God's honor is at stake, members of the church should pray that their pastor and their pastor's family would not fall prey to the world, to the flesh, or to the devil.

Can you see the necessity to pray for physical and spiritual protection for your leaders? Can you see the need to pray for deliverance from people who do not have faith? The two-edged sword principle applies here as well. Not only are we praying for our leaders for protection, but we pray also for ourselves that we would not be faithless or perverse or evil. When we are praying for our pastor to be delivered from faithless men, then we must be people of faith. As our pastors and leaders are protected from faithless people, then they are free to give us what we will discuss in the next chapter. Read on.

Chapter Four

A FEARLESS WORD

Ephesians 6:19-20 NIV
"Pray also for me, that whenever I speak, words may be given me so that I will fearlessly make known the mystery of the gospel, for which I am an ambassador in chains. Pray that I may declare it fearlessly, as I should."

It is so important for our leaders to be able to speak the truth to us. The apostle Paul asked for prayer for this, as shown in Ephesians 6:19-20. He wrote, "Pray also for me, that whenever I speak, words may be given me so that I will fearlessly make known the mystery of the gospel, for which I am an ambassador in chains. Pray that I may declare it fearlessly, as I should" (NIV).

We could look at several things in these two verses. We could talk about the mystery of the gospel or that Paul was an ambassador in chains. But for this study on praying for your pastor, there are two important requests that Paul makes. As a side note, I think it is important to note that when Paul has a prayer request, he is always explicit as to what he wants prayer for. It is never what we call "a special unspoken request," and it is always for prayer that activates the faith of the person praying. He was not afraid to be specific and neither should we. On the other hand, we need to be careful about who we ask to pray for us. We should only ask people we trust and who we know will pray in faith for us. Facebook, for this reason, is not the best place to ask for prayer. Pastors know who they can trust with a prayer request and as their congregation member you should be one of those trustworthy, faith-filled people. When you have a specific need, find people that you trust and ask them directly to pray for you.

The first prayer request that Paul makes in Ephesians 6:19 is, "Pray also for me, that whenever I speak, words may be given me." Now, looking at this in the natural, if Paul is speaking, then he is using words, right? He is not speaking gibberish, so he must be using words. But Paul is looking for a specific kind of word. Paul is asking that whenever he speaks, he would speak the *word* of the Lord. *Word* from the original Greek *logos*[12] is defined in *Strong's Concordance* as a decree, mandate, order, or the moral precepts given by God. *Logos* is not only the word about God, but it is His very words given to us. Paul is saying that he does not want to speak his opinions about a subject or issue, but that he wants to speak the word of God.

I have found out through the years that I can be pretty opinionated at times. As I am writing this, in my mind I can hear my wife give a hearty "AMEN." Though I have many opinions, I have also come to realize that nobody really wants to hear them. Well, maybe my close friends might be interested in my opinions, but they also have an expectation that my thoughts will be laced with a Biblical world view. What people really want from me is the word of God. My congregation wants the word of God. The now word. The prophetic word. They have the right to expect that I will decree, release a mandate, and order the moral precepts of God. 1 Thessalonians 2:13 says, "For this reason we also constantly thank God that when you received the word of God which you heard from us, you accepted it not as the word of men, but for what it really is, the word of God, which also performs its work in you who believe." People don't need the words of men; they need the logos of God to perform its work in them. I like the word *performs*. In the original language, it is the word *energeo*.[13] This is where we get the word energy from. *Energeo* means...

- to be operative
- be at work
- to put forth power

- to work for one
- to aid one
- to effect
- to display one's activity
- show oneself operative

I think it is safe to say that my opinions will not do that. These days, it is hard to get away from opinions. There is the old saying, "Opinions are like noses; everybody has one." The world has always had strong opinions, but lately, things have gotten more so. Every media outlet and every social media outlet is over-run with opinions. Even news agencies with their 24/7 news cycle on both sides of the political spectrum have turned into op-ed programs. Not only that, but because our feelings and emotions are so caught up in our opinions, it is no longer acceptable to have a different opinion than the prevailing winds. If you do, you will be demonized and called all kinds of evil, racist, hateful, stupid, even a Nazi. The left believes that everything the right says is evil. The right believes that everything the left says is stupid, and it goes on and on.

What we need are preachers that will preach the word of God and not their own op-ed pieces. Preachers who will decree, mandate, and order the truth of God. Your prayers can encourage your pastor to be that kind of preacher. The great theologian A.W. Tozer said, "We need preachers who preach that hell's still hot, heaven's still real, sin's still wrong and the Bible is God's Word." 2 Timothy 4:2 says, "Preach the word; be ready in season and out of season; reprove, rebuke, exhort, with great patience and instruction."

The word for *preach* here in the Greek is the word *kēryssō*,[14] and it means to be a herald, to proclaim. Heralding and proclaiming are not the same as teaching, although there can and should be an element of teaching in the preaching and preaching in the teaching. We used to say things like, "So-and-so is a great preacher; he can spit three rows back." Just because someone screams, shouts, spits, and carries a ten-pound Bible does not make him a preacher. A preacher proclaims the word of God with boldness and clarity. The second part of 2 Timothy

4:2 says, "Reprove, rebuke, exhort, with great patience and instruction." The New International Version translates it as "correct, rebuke and encourage." That is what real preaching does. Then it goes on to say, "with great patience and careful instruction." Obviously, that truth flies in the face of the prevailing winds of emotion and opinions. When there is relative truth or no truth in a society, then real truth is not generally received well.

Paul continues to say in 2 Timothy 4:3-4, "For the time will come when they will not endure sound doctrine; but wanting to have their ears tickled, they will accumulate for themselves teachers in accordance to their own desires, and will turn away their ears from the truth and will turn aside to myths." Paul seems to be talking about us in our time. Because of this, we need pastors that will preach the whole word of God and not just what people want to hear. A preacher who preaches uncompromised truth will be opened to all forms of attacks. 2 Peter 2:5 says that Noah was known as a preacher of righteousness, and for doing so, he was persecuted and ridiculed; that is, until it finally started to rain. That is why we need someone who will pray for us to preach an uncompromised word.

The second part of Paul's prayer request in Ephesians 6:19-20 says, "Pray that I may declare it fearlessly, as I should." In this passage, Paul uses the word fearlessly twice. Anything the Bible says once is important. When it says it twice, then it's really important. A Christian leader must be able to preach the word fearlessly without worrying about offending someone and without concern for the consequences of speaking against a Godless society. Your pastor should not be concerned about what people think or whether someone will leave the church because he/she preaches a strong word.

Do you know that there was a time in Jesus' ministry when the people began to leave Him? That's right. It happened when He started preaching things that some did not understand or misunderstood. In John chapter 6, Jesus proclaimed that He is the bread of life. He went on to say that they must eat His flesh and drink His blood. This sounded like cannibalism to them and it totally went against their Jewish practices. John 6:60 shows us their reaction. "Therefore, many of His disciples, when they heard this said, 'This is a difficult statement; who can listen to it'"? If we read on in verse 66, we see the mass exit. "As a result of this many of His disciples withdrew and were not walking with Him anymore." Yep, even Jesus lost people because of what He said.

No minister in his/her right mind wants to deliberately offend anybody, but even Jesus offended people. Sometimes we have to say hard things but true things. In Ephesians chapter 4, Paul teaches about the purpose of the five-fold ministry, those who are apostles, prophets, evangelists, pastors, and teachers. Their purpose is to bring the church into maturity. Ephesians 4:15 says, "But speaking the truth in love, we are to grow up in all aspects into Him who is the head, even Christ." The reason hard words need to be said is so that we grow up in all aspects. We cannot do that if we only hear words we want to hear.

The other side to this is that when we pray for our pastor to preach the word fearlessly, we cannot allow ourselves to get offended when they do preach the word fearlessly. We cannot be hypocrites with our prayers and think that their message does not apply to us. We must be open to what our leaders say and receive it as being what it actually is, the word of God at work in us. Do not let yourself get offended at the word of God no matter who the vessel is. Receive it. Apply it. Own it. Allow it to change you to be mature in Christ.

Chapter Five

OPEN DOORS

Colossians 4:3
"Praying at the same time for us as well, that God will open up to us a door for the word, so that we may speak forth the mystery of Christ, for which I have also been imprisoned."

Rapid growth, protection, a word from God, and fearlessness are the prayer requests from the apostle Paul that we have studied so far. Now we go to his next request, that God would open a door for the word. Colossians 4:3 says, "Praying at the same time for us as well, that God will open up to us a door for the word, so that we may speak forth the mystery of Christ, for which I have also been imprisoned." It is not enough to have a word, or to be fearless about it. There needs to be a place to speak it. There needs to be people to preach to. An open door could be many different things.

A. A new venue to preach or minister

If the vision of your church is from God, then it is a great vision and other people need to hear it. The four walls of your building cannot contain it. Often God will give your pastor a word that was meant to go beyond your ears only, and you must be open to that. Sometimes, this will mean new places for your pastor to preach or teach, maybe at a conference or a regional gathering. It can also mean publishing a book or producing a video.

B. New members

When we pray for open doors, we are also praying for new church members to hear the word. This goes along with our chapter on rapid growth. Two scriptures are an important part of my prayer life, and I encourage my congregation to pray them as well. The first one is Psalms 2:8, "Ask me, and I will make the nations your inheritance, the ends of the earth your possession" (NIV). What a great promise this is. The nations are our inheritance if we just ask. They belong to us in Christ. There are people in our city and region that God has designated to be a part of our church. As of 2017, there were 821,173 people in the greater Lehigh Valley. Can you imagine just how many nations are represented within? Those nations are our inheritance. It gives me chills just thinking about it.

Another verse is I confess daily is Acts 2:47, "Praising God and enjoying the favor of all the people. And the Lord added to their number daily those who were being saved" (NIV). I like to confess this scripture in the following way: "*We* are praising God and enjoying the favor of all the people. And the Lord added to *our* number daily those who are being saved."

Let me ask you a few questions. Is your church enjoying the favor of all the people? Does your pastor enjoy that favor? Let me remind you that the early church suffered tremendous persecution, yet Luke said that they enjoyed the favor of all the people. How could that be? Well, the previous three verses say, "They devoted themselves to the apostles' teaching and to fellowship, to the breaking of bread and to prayer. Everyone was filled with awe at the many wonders and signs performed by the apostles. All the believers were together and had everything in common. They sold property and possessions to give to anyone who had need. Every day they continued to meet together in the temple courts. They broke bread in their homes and ate together with glad and sincere hearts" (NIV). The early church was devoted to…

- The apostles teaching
- To fellowship

- Breaking of bread
- Prayer

What are you and your fellow church members devoted to? Let me ask you another question. When was the last time someone got saved in your church? Now I know that you have probably had new people visit from other churches. Maybe someone new to the area has hooked up with your church. That is transfer growth, from church to church. But I am talking about someone getting saved right in your church service. You can pray for that to happen, and their heart becomes another open door. That leads us to our next type of open door.

C. New believers

New believers are a completely different kind of open door. That is a door that has never been opened before. They are completely unaware of doctrines, rituals, and theology. Some of them have probably never even picked up a Bible before let alone understand all the things that we take for granted because we have heard it so many times before.

I know someone who had just gotten saved and started coming to our church. A guest speaker was ministering who quoted a scripture that Jesus had said. Now, it is not important for this story what Jesus said, and honestly, I do not really remember. But what is important, and was very revealing to me, was that when the minister quoted it, she said that she knew it was Jesus who said it because it was in red letters. Well, the girl that had just gotten saved said, sort of under her breath, "Oh, that's what the red letters mean." She had no clue. Well, everybody had a good laugh about it, but that moment changed the way I prepare a message. I began to realize that not everybody knows our Christianese. Do you realize that your pastor must preach a message that can be understood by people of all walks of life? Young, old, rich, poor. Laborer, businessperson, man, women. No two people are the same. Can you see how they need your prayers? But they do not need your pity prayers. You know what I mean? "Oh, poor Pastor, he has so much work to do and no one to help him do it. Please help your humble servant Lord." Yuck! Don't pray the problem; pray the solution. The solution is to pray for open doors for your pastor and the ministry. And another solution would be for you to get in there and help the pastor with the work of the ministry. There is one more door we need to pray for.

D. The door of your heart

If your heart is not open to your pastor's input, how can you pray for any other open door? We always like to see someone else squirm under the anointing. You can tell when someone is getting their mail read, so to speak. But what about those times when you feel like the pastor is just talking to you? Do you get offended? Do you shut yourself off to what God wants to say to you? Hebrews 12:15 says, "See to it that no one comes short of the grace of God; that no root of bitterness springing up causes trouble, and by it many be defiled." Do not be offended by the word of God or by the messenger who brings it. Do not let bitterness take root in your life and defile your relationship with the man or women of God. Remain humble and open to teaching. Allow maturity to take root and not bitterness.

Another reason that we want to pray for an open door is because there is always opposition to the word of God. In fact, the very first sin that occurred was because the serpent said to Eve, "Did God really say?" The enemy is always challenging the word of God. He did it then, and he still does it today. The apostle Paul said in 1 Corinthians 16:9, "Because a great door for effective work has opened to me, and there are many who oppose me" (NIV). There was a great door for an effective work, but there was also opposition. What the New International Version translates as opposition, the original Greek calls adversary. We do not want there to be adversaries from outside the church or from inside the church. Pray for open doors. Be an open door. Encourage your pastor to walk through those doors and make sure you walk with them. Be like Aaron and Hur and hold up your Moses' hands in prayer and support.[15]

Chapter Six

CLARITY

Colossians 4:4
"That I may make it clear in the way I ought to speak."

Clarity is the key to communication. Communication is one of the primary jobs of a pastor, five-fold minister, or any leader. Colossians 4:4 is a continuation from the previous prayer request. You remember in verse three Paul asked for prayer for an open door for ministry. Verse four takes it to another level. Look at what he says in Colossians 4:4, "That I may make it *clear* in the way I ought to speak" (emphasis mine).

What good is a message if nobody understands what you just said. As a pastor, I have had many opportunities to counsel with people. Husbands and wives, seniors, single people, teenagers, even children. Not only that, but I get to teach them from the pulpit every week. They all have one thing in common; they are all different. They are come from different walks of life with different reference points and different paradigms. I give the same message to all these different types of people. A pastor needs to communicate one vision to many different types of people from different walks of life.

- Farmer
- Businessperson
- Housewife
- Single mom

- Senior
- Professional
- Student
- Child

All of them see things differently and hear things differently. I am not complaining. It is the job I have been called to. We are told we are in the age of communication, but seldom is there any real, meaningful communication taking place. We call it social networking, but it really isn't. It is social *not* working. Think of all the major resources we have which allows us to communicate with one another.

- Texting
- Facebook
- Messenger
- Twitter
- LinkedIn
- Instagram
- Email
- 24/7 news cycle

With all those resources at our disposal, we are more divided than ever before. From an article posted on oprah.com titled "Social Not Working: The Perils of Too Much Communication,"[16] it states, "'It can be exhilarating, at least at first, to connect with long-lost friends,' says network science expert Steven Strogatz, PhD, a professor of applied mathematics at Cornell University. But the downside, he worries, is growing confusion between our weak ties (people who might be useful in referring us to a good dentist or helping us find a job) and our strong ties (those we are very close to). 'The distinction between genuine friends and acquaintances is becoming blurred. Users are spending time maintaining relationships with people they don't really care about.'"

Clarity is key. It amazes me that, I know what I was thinking when I said it, and I know what I said when I said it, but that is not what some people heard me say. It always comes back to me sooner or later. I might see something that someone shared on Facebook Sunday afternoon about what they think I said, but what they heard is not even close to what I said. I wonder, where did they get that from? What church service were they even in? Or I might think I had a great counseling session with someone, but I come to find out that they did not understand me at all. We must be clear about what we are saying, and our congregation can pray for us that we will have clarity when we speak.

When Paul asked his followers to pray that he would speak with *clarity*,[17] he asked that he would be able to preach a message or teach something that would be apparent, made manifest, and understandable. No misunderstandings. No misquoting or taking out of context. He wants his message to be plain and recognizable. The prophet Habakkuk said it this way, Habakkuk 2:2, "Then the Lord replied: "Write down the revelation and *make it plain* on tablets so that a herald may run with it" (NIV) (emphasis mine).

According to the *Theological Wordbook of The Old Testament*, the phrase *make it plain*[18] is described as, "writing on tablets of stone made clear and distinct or to write upon tablets which is *legible at a hurried glance*. In figurative use, the verb means to make clear by explaining" (emphasis mine). This implies that no matter who hears it or sees it, no matter what the circumstance, they should be able to understand the vision and run with it. One thing that always amazes me is how people do not hear what you say, they hear what they feel.

Pastors and leaders, do your people know the vision of your ministry? Do you communicate it in such a way that people from all walks of life can apply the word to their lives? As a preacher, your main role is that of a communicator. One dictionary definition of a *communicator*[19] is a person who conveys information or knowledge to others. This means giving more than just information. The hearer must be able to understand what you are saying. Are you preaching your grand revelation, but it is going over the heads of everyone who is listening? Be a good clear communicator. Do not be ambivalent about what you say. Your people's lives depend on your clarity. Communicate the vision clearly.

This again is a two-edged sword, because when we pray for our pastor to have clarity, we are also praying that we would correctly hear the message. The last words of the prophet Hosea in Hosea 14:9 says, "Whoever is wise, let him understand these things; whoever is discerning, let him know them. For the ways of the Lord are right, and the righteous will walk in them, but transgressors will stumble in them." You see, you have a responsibility in this as well to be wise and discerning with what you hear. You need to understand what your leader is saying. As you pray for them for clarity, make sure your mind and heart are open to receive the word. A key to this is listening. Listen to what is said. Take the word for face value. Tune out the rest of the world and pay attention. Forget about what you are going to do after church; it will still be there. Distractions, things like falling asleep, excessive yawning, babies crying, people getting up and moving around during the message, will hinder you from hearing the word clearly. I have even seen people clipping their nails during the service or clicking their ball point pens. I am not trying to be excessively critical. Distractions happen and sometimes you have no control over them, but come on man, have some respect for the word of God and the house of God.

Chapter Seven

INTEGRITY

Hebrews 13:18
"Pray for us, for we are sure that we have a good conscience, desiring to conduct ourselves honorably in all things."

Having a good conscience and having integrity go hand-in-hand. In fact, a good conscience is a by-product of having integrity. All true leaders must develop integrity in their lives. You would think that concept would be a given, but you would be wrong. Nothing is a given in our walk with God. Everything needs to be watched over with a fine-toothed comb. It's when we start to ignore things, that the drift comes. A person never falls away immediately. Falling away is a process. It is gradual and almost unnoticeable at first. In fact, we rarely notice it ourselves, but those that are close to us begin to see things. James describes the process of falling away in James 1:14-15, "Temptation comes from our own desires, which entice us and drag us away. These desires give birth to sinful actions. And when sin is allowed to grow, it gives birth to death" (NLT). Most people blame the devil for temptation, but James says that temptation comes from our own desires. Did you get that? Temptation comes from us. The next step in this drifting away is that our own desires entice us and drag us away. The concept of dragging away is the drift. We do not just fall off the cliff of sin. It is always a slow, gradual experience. It is like boiling a frog in water. If you place the frog in hot water, it will jump out. But if you place it in cold water and gradually turn up the heat, the frog gets used to it, and soon you have boiled frog's legs. Those selfish desires that cause us to fade away will eventually turn into sinful actions. If not corrected, it will lead to death. In fact, James says that it gives birth to death. In other words, it is a living death. A spiritual zombie. Do you know anybody like that? It does not matter if it is a physical death or a spiritual death. One is as bad as the other.

Song of Solomon 2:15 says, "Catch the foxes for us, the little foxes that are ruining the vineyards, while our vineyards are in blossom." The little things are what creates big problems for us. There was a popular saying that I believe contributed to a generational drift in our churches, "Don't sweat the small stuff." That means do not worry about minor issues or problems. While we do not want to worry about things, we do need to give our attention to the small stuff. These are the things that our conscience should keep us from doing, if we have a good conscience. If our conscience is not good, then, "Houston, we have a problem." Paul says this to Timothy in 1 Timothy 4:2, "Speaking lies in hypocrisy, having their own conscience seared with a hot iron" (NKJV). If one's conscience is seared, it literally means it has been cauterized. It has been rendered insensitive. That kind of conscience does not work properly. It has developed spiritual scar tissue which has dulled the sense of right and wrong. Just like the hide of an animal branded with a branding iron becomes numb to any further pain, so the heart of an individual with a seared conscience becomes numb to moral pain.

So, what is your conscience like? Every time I think about the word conscience, I'm reminded of the old Bugs Bunny cartoon where he is facing a moral decision. An angel appears on his right shoulder and tells him to do the right thing. The devil appears on his left shoulder and tries to tempt him to do the wrong thing. Bugs' response is always, "If I dooed' it, I get a whippin'. I dooed' it." You see, Bugs knew that he would eventually have to pay the consequences for doing what he knew he should not do, but the instant gratification was too much for him to resist. Though that is a humorous look on conscience, reality is a bit more complicated. What makes it even more complicated is the fact that conscience and truth are so relative in our society that it is a wonder that anyone knows the right thing to do. The Bible teaches a truth-centered conscience instead of a feelings-centered one. Proverbs 23:7 says, "For as he thinks in his heart, so is he. 'Eat and drink!' he says to you, but his heart is not with you" (NKJV).

Your conscience is what you think about in your heart. That's right, I said think *in your heart*. Did you know your that heart thinks? Jesus knew it when He said in Matthew 9:4, "And Jesus knowing their thoughts said, "Why are you thinking evil in your hearts?" The word *thinking* in Proverbs 23:7 is *sha'ar*,[20] in the original language. It means to split open, reason out, calculate, reckon, estimate. Now I am not sure what split open has to do with this. Maybe it is referring to opening our heart to something. It is probably why Solomon said to guard your heart.[21] The rest of the definition of *sha'ar* is clear. It is talking about figuring things out. You could rephrase Proverbs 23:7 another way, "The way you reason out, calculate, reckon and estimate in your heart, that's what you become." That is what you will do. That is what you will think. That is why a person that does not have a Biblical world view is a slave to their own feelings. Their conscience will never be dependable and sure.

Let us look at 1 Timothy 4:2 in The New Living Translation, "These people are hypocrites and liars, and their consciences are dead." I cannot think of anything worse than a leader whose conscience is dead. The previous verse is just as damning. Paul says in 1 Timothy 4:1, "But the Spirit explicitly says that in later times some will fall away from the faith, paying attention to deceitful spirits and doctrines of demons." Wow! There are plenty of deceitful spirits and doctrines of demons out there trying to get the attention of your pastor. Pray for him/her. Pray that they have a good conscience. A clear conscience. Pray that they conduct themselves honorably. Pray that they live in such a way that they honor Holy Spirit with their daily walk.

There is another scripture that has become crucial in my daily devotions and I confess it over myself every day. It helps me to be proactive in preventing my conscience from being seared. You would do well to do the same for yourself and for your leader. Philippians 4:8-9 says, "Finally, brethren, whatever is true, whatever is honorable, whatever is right, whatever is pure, whatever is lovely, whatever is of good repute, if there is any excellence and if anything is worthy of praise, dwell on these things. The things you have learned and received and heard and seen in me, practice these things, and the God of peace will be with you."

There are eight parts to this preventative maintenance of your heart. I call them "the eight whatevers." It is kind of a twist on some attitudes of the younger generation. I hear them say it all the time, "Whatever." In their case, it means, "I hear what you're saying, but I really don't care. You know nothing and I know everything. Just go away and let me do it my way." Of course, none of us have that attitude, right? But in our case, *whatever* means if there is anything you can think of that is true, right, pure, lovely, of good repute, excellent, and worthy of praise, then that's what you should be thinking about. Not only thinking about them but dwelling on them. The Greek word for dwell is *logizomai*,[22] and it has some interesting origins. It is a verb in the middle voice. When the Greek middle voice verb form is used, the subject of the verb is seen as acting upon itself or for its own benefit. *Logizomai* means to take an inventory of something. To reckon it. To reason it out. You see, it is a bit more than just having a passing thought. It is time and effort spent considering what is true, right, pure, lovely, of good repute, excellent, and worthy of praise. That is what keeps us out of trouble. Pray those words for your leader. Let us look a little deeper at the eight whatevers. I believe that every church member should expect that their leaders would dwell on these things and be a model of them so that you can follow.

Whatever is...

1. True — when something is what it says it is

This is more than just telling the truth or speaking the truth in love. Truth is the very foundation of integrity. It means that you are what you say you are. Just like the incident with Jesus and the fig tree,[23] what you advertise is what you are. Why did Jesus curse the fig tree? Because it was advertising fruit, but it did not have any. Literally the reverse of truth in advertising.

2. Noble — honorable of deeds

Noble is a word that we as Americans do not really understand. It speaks of royalty. We do not have royalty in America and that is why it is so hard for us to grasp that we are royalty in Christ. But there is more to it than that. It means that you know what the right thing is to do, and you do it. You honor your commitments. You do not quit. You are what you want your congregation to be. You pay your bills on time. Do you get the picture?

3. Right — innocent, faultless, guiltless

This does not mean that you are right all the time. It means that you are in right standing with God, your church, and your community. It means that you cannot "flirt" with the world. You must remain apart from it. If you need to ask the question, "Can I get away with this?" then do not do it. If you think you can do it and apologize later, you have already started to drift.

4. Pure — clean and set apart

Purity is the essence of holiness. Holiness is not so much what you do or do not do. It is more about being separate from the world. God is holy. As Isaiah saw and heard the angels cry out, "Holy, holy, holy,"[24] he understood that they were saying, "Separate, separate, separate." What is God separate from? Everything. He is separate from everything that He created. He can interact with us and not be changed by the interaction. He is all knowing, ever present, all powerful, and He never changes. Do you know anybody else like that? When God says in Leviticus 11:44a, "I am the Lord your God; consecrate yourselves and *be holy, because I am holy*" (NIV, emphasis mine). He is saying that He wants us to be just like him. That word *holy* is the same holy that Isaiah heard the angels cry out.

5. Lovely — someone who loves well

Lovely in this case does not mean good looking. Sorry guys. It is the word *prosphilēs*[25] and it comes from the word *phileo* which we know means brotherly love. It means friendly. Someone once said, "People aren't looking for a friendly church, they are looking for friends." I believe the pastor and the leadership sets the tone for this to take place in their members.

6. Admirable — of good report or reputation

Don't you want to hear good reports from the community about your church and your pastor? I think it's interesting that Acts 2:47 says that early church was "praising God and having favor with all the people. And the Lord added to the church daily those who were being saved." I believe there is a correlation between favor and church growth. They had favor with people, all the people not just with each other. Because of that favor, people were getting saved. When was the last time you saw growth because people got saved? Not just transfer growth. Your prayers for your pastor can help produce that. If you are a pastor reading this, I would like to ask you a couple of questions. Who do you admire? Why do you admire them? Do you think that you give anybody cause to admire you?

7. Excellent — moral excellence

We are all bombarded with the views of a world that has no morality. Anything goes.

In fact, people try to outdo one another in their quest to become morally bankrupt. Alexis de Tocqueville said, "Liberty cannot be established without morality, nor morality without faith."[26] In our quest for freedom, even in the church, we are systematically removing any semblance of morality and truth because we misunderstand freedom. We are not free to do; we are free to become. Grace does not give us the freedom to do what we want when we want. It gives us the enabling power to do what is necessary to become what God wants us to be. Galatians 5:1 says, "It was for freedom that Christ set us free; therefore, keep standing firm and do not be subject again to a yoke of slavery." That yoke of slavery is a slavery to our own desires. Grace gives us the power to stand firm and not be subject to the yoke again. We must pray for our leaders that they stand true to the faith, to a Biblical morality, and to the vision that God has called them to.

8. Praiseworthy — commendable

What is praiseworthy? We tend to measure our success by comparing ourselves with other people, and pastors are no exception. One of the first things pastors ask each other in conversation is how many people attend our churches. If we have 1000 people in Sunday attendance, and the pastor we are talking to has 1,100 people, then we are not as successful as they are. I would like to offer a different metric for success. Obeying the will of God. Many of us pastors like to think that we are called to pastor a mega-church, but the fact is that most of us never will. Some of us are called to lead small churches. Does that mean that those pastors are less successful? Less praiseworthy? What about a leader who remains faithful to their spouse for 50 or 60 years? I think that is praiseworthy. What about the leader who is called to pastor a little country church and remains faithful to their congregation for 40 or 50 years? Pastors need prayer to remain true to the calling of God on their lives. It is easy to get caught up in the whole church growth mentality and lose the purpose that God originally intended for them. Now, if you are called to pastor a mega-church, then do so with humility and with the grace of God. But you should never look down on your calling.

Leaders need the prayers of the saints to live their lives with integrity and honor so that they will bring glory to God and not disgrace Him as so many have done before.

Chapter Eight

PRAYING THE WORD

2 Timothy 3:16
"All Scripture is inspired by God and profitable for teaching, for reproof, for correction, for training in righteousness."

We have just studied six prayer requests which when prayed will bring a fresh power to your church and ministry and bring you closer to your pastor. They will also keep you from some of the pitfalls that even church members can fall into. But wait, there's more! There are more three great scriptures that I pray over myself daily that have become a very important part of my prayers for other ministers and churches. Let me share them with you now.

Isaiah 11:2 says, "The Spirit of the Lord will rest on Him, the spirit of wisdom and understanding, the spirit of counsel and strength, the spirit of knowledge and the fear of the Lord." This verse is often called the seven spirits of God. I understand where that terminology comes from but let me make a point. God has *one* Spirit. In fact, He is spirit. John 4:24 says "God is spirit, and those who worship Him must worship in spirit and truth." Wisdom, understanding, counsel, strength, knowledge, and the fear of the Lord are result of the Spirit of the Lord resting on Him. Let us look at this a little deeper.

In order to have a better understanding about this we let us look at the previous verse. Isaiah 11:1 says, "Then a shoot will spring from the stem of Jesse, and a branch from his roots will bear fruit." We know that this is a prophecy of Jesus. The stem of Jesse is David. Jesus is the shoot from the stem of Jesse. Acts 13:22-23 gives us further revelation on this point. It says, "After He had removed him, He raised up David to be their king, concerning whom He also testified and said, 'I have found David the son of Jesse, a man after My heart, who will do all My will.' From the descendants of this man, according to promise, God has brought to Israel a Savior, Jesus." Now, what does that have to do with our spiritual leaders? Well remember, we are talking about the five-fold ministry who are the leadership gifts that Jesus gave to men in Ephesians 4:12, "For the equipping of the saints for the work of service, to the building up of the body of Christ." These five-fold ministers are our leaders. We should have an expectation that wisdom, understanding, counsel, strength, knowledge, and the fear of the Lord rests upon our leaders. We can also ensure that all six of these attributes rest on them as we pray specifically for them for our pastors. Let us study all six a little deeper.

A.   Wisdom and understanding

Wouldn't it be great if our leaders had some wisdom and understanding? There is an anointing of wisdom for leaders. I am not just talking about spiritual leaders but leaders in general. Political, business, teachers, arts and entertainment, sports, media. In any area where there is influence, there is leadership. John Maxwell says that leadership is influence,[27] and I agree. Wisdom is more than talk. We hear a lot of talk in all areas of life but not much wisdom. People love to hear themselves talk but nobody else wants to listen. I am reminded of the E. F. Hutton commercial years ago that had lots of people talking in a room with nobody responding, and then E. F. Hutton steps up to speak and everybody stops talking and pays attention. The caption says, "When E. F. Hutton speaks, people listen." Wisdom causes people to listen.

Wisdom is a recurring theme in the Bible. The dictionary definition of *wisdom*[28] is the ability to discern or judge what is true, right, or lasting, insight. The Bible speaks a lot about wisdom. The book of Proverbs is probably the greatest concentration of wisdom ever written. One of the most well-known of these verses is Proverbs 1:7 which says,

"The fear of the Lord is the beginning of knowledge; fools despise wisdom and instruction." That word *fear* in Hebrew is a feminine noun. I think it is interesting that this is a feminine noun, because throughout the book of Proverbs, Solomon and others speak of wisdom also in the feminine voice. Proverbs 1:20 says, "Wisdom shouts in the street, *she* lifts her voice in the square" (emphasis mine). The word for *wisdom* is *chokmah*.[29] The *Theological Wordbook of the Old Testament* has a lot to say about this word.

> *The essential idea of this Hebrew word represents a manner of thinking and attitude concerning life's experiences, including matters of general interest and basic morality. These concerns relate to prudence in secular affairs, skills in the arts, moral sensitivity, and experience in the ways of the Lord. The wisdom of the Old Testament, however, is quite distinct from other ancient world views although the format of wisdom literature is like that of other cultures. Reflected in Old Testament wisdom is the teaching of a personal God who is holy and just and who expects those who know him to exhibit his character in the many practical affairs of life. This perfect blend of the revealed will of a holy God with the practical human experiences of life is also distinct from secular wisdom."*[30]

You can pray for that kind of wisdom for your pastor. All leaders who are true shepherds desire and need this wisdom from God. Pray for it. Declare it. Believe that your pastor is speaking the wisdom of God when he speaks to you.

B. Counsel and might

When we think of a pastor having the spirit of counsel, we think about someone who can counsel others with wisdom and knowledge. A minister of the gospel needs to have the necessary wisdom to counsel, to know when to confront, be able to mediate, and to discern the individual pastoral needs of those in his congregation. This is an all-encompassing and a recurring need. A pastor needs to have empathy but will also be able to tell you the truth in love. Love should be the motivation for this empathy; every shepherd should love their sheep.

Counseling can be a pretty tricky thing for pastors. It has been my unfortunate experience as a pastor that the people with whom I have counseled the most are the ones who eventually leave the church. There have been times that I have invested many hours of counseling and instruction with some people only to have them leave after it is all said and done. Maybe they are embarrassed to have discussed such deep problems with someone else. Maybe they feel like their pastor will use the information against them. Sometimes, they just do not want to do what they are counseled to do, but people will leave more often than you think. Most pastors, including myself, are not professional counselors. They are visionaries, but it is part of our job description as a pastor to counsel with people.

The Hebrew word for *counsel*[31] means advice. It also means to give purpose. Part of counseling someone is to advise them on what their purpose is, or the reasoning behind what they are going though. Romans 8:28 says, "And we know that God causes all things to work together for good to those who love God, to those who are called according to His purpose." We are called to counsel people on the goodness of God, and what His purpose is. I cannot count the people who have asked me what I thought the will of God was for their lives. Of course, I can't tell them what God's specific will for them is, but I can help guide them and provide them with the opportunity to find out what that is.

There is another aspect of this phrase *the spirit of counsel* and that is this; the counsel and company our leaders keep. We need to pray for our leaders that they surround themselves with good, wise, and apostolic counsel. We also need to pray that they keep the counsel of God. They need to seek the will of God for the community they pastor. That means that they need to spend adequate time in His presence, in His word, and in prayer for the people they shepherd. It is important that pastors and leaders not have their schedules so filled up with meetings that they cannot schedule enough time to meet with the Lord. Jesus Himself spoke about the importance of spending time with God. In Luke chapter 10, we find Jesus teaching in Mary and Martha's house. It gives the picture of Martha running around like a chicken with its head cut off taking care of business while Mary remained at the feet of Jesus being taught. Martha was not having any of it. To her, Mary looked like she was being lazy just sitting there while Martha did all the work. Jesus gently rebuked her. Verses 41-42 say, "But the Lord answered and said to her, 'Martha, Martha, you are worried and bothered about so many things; but only one thing is necessary, for Mary has chosen the good part, which shall not be taken away from her.'" What part did Mary chose? She chose to spend time in the presence of Jesus.

I know how Martha must have felt, for I am a detail-oriented person myself. I am not naturally given to extended times in God's presence. I am always looking to do the next thing on my to-do list. In fact, I have often felt guilty about having to make spending time in His presence a part of that to-do list, as if it is a chore or something. But I would rather schedule it in, than not do it at all. Don't get me wrong, I have sweet times in His presence daily, but if I don't make it happen, life goes on and on until I realize that I haven't spent time in His presence for a while. I do lots of important ministry stuff, but the most important thing is spending time with Him. That time with the Father is what will produce the next aspect of the Spirit of the Lord being upon us, and that is the spirit of might.

Isaiah prophesied that along with the spirit of counsel would be the spirit of might. It is clear to me that the spirit of might is the result of keeping counsel with God. The meaning of the Hebrew word for *might*[32] is valor, victory, force, mastery, might, power, and strength. I particularly like the word *valor*. It reminds me of King David's mighty men.[33] Those men were celebrated though out the land, but they were not always that way. When David fled from Saul, he hid in a place called the cave of Adullam. This is where these mighty men started to gather to David. But they were not mighty at the beginning. In fact, they were quite the opposite. 1 Samuel 22:1-2 says, "So David departed from there and escaped to the cave of Adullam; and when his brothers and all his father's household heard of it, they went down there to him. Everyone who was in distress, and everyone who was in debt, and everyone who was discontented gathered to him; and he became captain over them. Now there were about four hundred men with him." Not the best start for an army. But David took the men God gave him and with the spirit of wisdom and knowledge, counsel and might, he created this army of mighty men. Don't you want your pastor to have the ability to create a church that is a mighty army in the region God has placed you? Your prayers for him can help accomplish this. Now, there are two more aspects of Isaiah 11:2 that we must look at.

C. Knowledge and the fear of the Lord

Now, knowledge is related to wisdom, but it is a bit different. Knowledge is information gained through experience, reasoning, or acquaintance. Knowledge can exist without wisdom, but not the other way around. You can be knowledgeable without being wise. Knowledge is knowing how to use a gun; wisdom is knowing when to use it and when to keep it holstered. There is a big difference. Wisdom is the ability to put into practice the knowledge you have from the Lord. It is great to have knowledge, but if you do not know how to apply it, it is just information. We need leaders that have more than just good ideas and big dreams. Don't misunderstand me, leaders should have dream and visions, but they should also have knowledge to know how to accomplish those grand ideas. They should know how to find the right people for the right jobs. They should know how to make alliances and how to work together with people to accomplish the vision that God gave them. No vision can stand alone. We must pray for our leaders that they would have wisdom and knowledge from the Lord.

This kind of knowledge is more than just understanding how to do stuff. It has to do with the next phrase *the fear of the Lord*. This is not necessarily knowledge *and* the fear of the Lord, as our English translation states. It is more like the knowledge *of* the fear of the Lord. Your pastor must have a grasp of the fear of the Lord for his life and yours.

It is what keeps us all living a holy life, separated unto the Lord. Now, with the spreading of the hyper-grace doctrine, knowledge of the fear of the Lord becomes even more important. 2 Timothy 4:3-4 says, "For the time will come when they will not endure sound doctrine; but wanting to have their ears tickled, they will accumulate for themselves teachers in accordance to their own desires and will turn away their ears from the truth and will turn aside to myths."

I believe that one of the greatest errors spreading through the church today is this false grace doctrine. Nobody explains this error better than my good friend Dr. William Luffman. He explains it this way in his book entitled *Disgraceful Grace*.

> *The emphasis is on the grace of God to the exclusive of critical, time-tested, biblically sound doctrine especially where repentance and the confession of sin are concerned. It is built on the notion that all sin ever committed or to be committed, past, present, and future, has already been forgiven. With that thought in mind, it excludes the need to repent and confess sin before the Father. It states that any return to God to confess sin or repent is to go back under the law of Moses, which we have been delivered from. It even minimizes the teachings of Jesus to the degree that His words were not meant for the post-resurrection believer. It also concludes that any attempt to correct sinful believers is legalistic and diminishes the work of grace. These beliefs are entirely erroneous, out of context, and out of order with sound doctrine. Repentance is throughout the Bible. Before the law of Moses, during the law of Moses, and after the law of Moses! Repentance renews grace."*[34]

Having the fear of the Lord does not mean that we are afraid of Him. It is also much more than reverence for Him. We are afraid of Him because of His goodness. His goodness is His faithfulness to all generations. We are a part of "all generations." The fear of the Lord is the very basis of our trust in Him. I have heard people downplay the idea of the fear of the Lord saying that it is just reverence. It is much more.

The fear of the Lord is a fear of offending Him. It is knowing that our thoughts, words, and action have consequences, and that one of the consequences is grieving Holy Spirit. That does not mean we will never make any mistakes or sin. The fear of the Lord causes us to have a certain response to God when we fail. I would like to quote something from my first book entitled *The Key of David*. In it, I teach about the character traits from the life of David that caused him to be a man after God's own heart. I believe it is vital to get a true understanding of the fear of the Lord. From chapter 9 of the book, I write,

> *Acts 13:22 "After removing Saul, he made David their king. God testified concerning him: 'I have found David son of Jesse, a man after my own heart; he will do everything I want him to do'" (NIV).*

> *In the last chapter, we discussed briefly Saul's disobedience being the reason why Saul never fulfilled God's destiny. We see in Acts 13:22 that God said David would do everything God told him to do. David made some serious errors in his life; he committed adultery with Bathsheba, murdered her husband Uriah to cover it up, acted impulsively trying to bring the ark to Jerusalem, and much more. But the thing that distinguished him from everybody else is that he would always make it right with God. It was his willingness to repent before the Lord and fall upon God's grace for forgiveness. This pleased God. David didn't always do the right thing, but he always took responsibility for his own actions before the Lord. Not only that, but his repentance was not for the sake of man, but for God. Look at his attitude in Psalm 25:11, "For the sake of your name, Lord, forgive my iniquity, though it is great" (NIV).*

> *David was afraid of dishonoring the name of the Lord. The Hebrew word for the phrase "the sake of your name" is shem, and it means "your reputation Lord." The name Shem was given to one of Noah's sons, and it means fame, glory and by implication honor, authority, and character. David was more concerned about the excellency of God's name than his own. I really believe this is the best description of "the fear of the Lord." Being more concerned about His reputation than ours.*[35]

We need pastors and leaders that are not so consumed with their own reputation but are consumed with the thought that they do not want to offend God. As worshippers, when we give God the glory, we are saying, "God, your fame, glory, honor and authority are more important than mine. Give us hearts like David. Make us people that are after God's own heart and not ours." But wait, there's more!

The second great verse that I confess daily is Isaiah 11:3 which says, "And He will delight in the fear of the Lord." To delight in something is to find great pleasure in it. To delight in the fear of the Lord is to take pleasure in the fact that you are pleasing God. Don't you think that would be a great attribute to have? Pleasing God is my delight, and I hope most pastors would agree.

And the third great verse I confess daily is Jeremiah 3:15 which says, "Then I will give you shepherds after my own heart, who will feed you on knowledge and understanding." The Lord is saying that it is He that is raising up and providing shepherds after his own heart. God is the one who has blessed and called pastors with the talents, skills, and heart that the Lord wants for his people. This verse also states that God is the one who gives shepherds and leaders the food for the sheep; in other words, He gives pastors the knowledge and understanding that they need to feed the sheep. The church needs these kinds of leaders.

Hebrews 13:17 says, "Have confidence in your leaders and submit to their authority, because they keep watch over you as those who must give an account. Do this so that their work will be a joy, not a burden, for that would be of no benefit to you" (NIV). As you pray for your pastor, and as you line up in agreement with the prayers you are praying, you will help your pastor and your congregation succeed in ministry.

Chapter Nine

LET'S START PRAYING

1 Timothy 2:1-2
"First of all, then, I urge that entreaties and prayers, petitions and thanksgivings, be made on behalf of all men, for kings and all who are in authority, so that we may lead a tranquil and quiet life in all godliness and dignity."

I have been able to teach the message in this book to many churches, including my own, and have seen some excellent results getting congregations to pray for their pastors and leaders. Something that I do at the end of my message is to call people up to the altar to pray for their pastor. I have them come up and surround their leaders, then I lead them in prayer using these scriptures. I ask them to repeat the prayers after me just to get them started in the practice of praying for their pastor. It is one thing to learn about it, it is another thing to begin right away putting into practice what they've just learned. In this final chapter, I would like to guide you through some simple prayers based on these six main scriptures so that you will get some experience praying the word for your own pastors. As you read these scriptures and prayers, speak them out loud. Use them until you can formulate your own prayers based on these scriptures. So, here we go.

1. **2 Thessalonians 3:1**

    "Finally, brethren, pray for us that the word of the Lord will spread rapidly and be glorified, just as it did also with you."

Father, I thank you for my pastor and my leaders. I pray that the word that they preach would spread rapidly through our community. I pray that the vision of our church would spread throughout our region, be recognized as the word of the Lord, and be glorified as it is with us. I pray that the word of God would spread rapidly, and that our church would grow rapidly according to Your word.

2. **2 Thessalonians 3:2**

    "And that we will be rescued from perverse and evil men; for not all have faith."

I pray for protection for my leaders. I ask that you protect them from faithless people. From people who are wicked, evil, and out-of-sorts with Your church. Surround our pastor with faithful men and women, people who will run with the vision of the church. People who will hold their hands up like Aaron and Hur did for Moses. Help me to be one of those people. Cause me to be a help and encouragement to my pastor.

3. **Ephesians 6:19-20**

    "Pray also for me, that whenever I speak, words may be given me so that I will fearlessly make known the mystery of the gospel, for which I am an ambassador in chains. Pray that I may declare it fearlessly, as I should" (NIV).

Lord, speak to my pastor. Give him/her the word of the Lord for us and our community. Give them a boldness to preach Your word. Do not let them be afraid or worried to speak the truth in love to us. Father help me to not get offended by what they say but cause me to embrace Your word and grow from it. Help my pastor to preach the full gospel at all times.

4. Colossians 4:3

> *"Praying at the same time for us as well, that God will open up to us a door for the word, so that we may speak forth the mystery of Christ, for which I have also been imprisoned."*

Father, I pray that You would open doors for my pastor to preach and minister. Cause new areas of ministry to open for them. Let new hearts be open to the mystery of Christ. Bring in new believers to become new disciples. Lord, I open my heart to receive the word. I declare that my heart is fertile ground for planting Your word.

5. Colossians 4:4

> *"That I may make it clear in the way I ought to speak."*

Lord, I thank you that my pastor is a great communicator. Cause the word and the vision that my pastor speaks be spoken with clarity so that all will hear and understand. Make it so plain that people from all walks of life will hear and apply it to their lives willingly. Let the word that they preach be full of wisdom, knowledge, counsel, might, and the fear of the Lord.

6. Hebrews 13:18

> *"Pray for us, for we are sure that we have a good conscience, desiring to conduct ourselves honorably in all things."*

I pray for my pastor and leaders to have a clear conscience and to always do the right thing even when it is hard. Create in them a heart of integrity and a Godly character so that they will honor You as they are examples of faith to us. Help me to honor that integrity by becoming an example myself as I run with the vision of my church.

I pray that as you pray these prayers, and as you add other scriptures that Lord may show you to pray, that you will get them deep into your spirit, make them a part of you so that they activate your faith, and become a great support to your leaders. As you support them, they will continue to be encouraged and help you move forward in your walk with God. Amen!

Endnotes

Chapter One

1 "G3402–mimētēs–Strong's Greek Lexicon (NASB)." Blue Letter Bible. Accessed 3 Sep, 2018. https://www.blueletterbible.org//lang/lexicon/lexicon.cfm?Strongs=G3402&t=NASB

Chapter Two

2 "G4335–proseuchē–Strong's Greek Lexicon (NASB)." Blue Letter Bible. Accessed 4 Sep, 2018. https://www.blueletterbible.org//lang/lexicon/lexicon.cfm?Strongs=G4335&t=NASB

3 "G3056–logos–Strong's Greek Lexicon (NASB)." Blue Letter Bible. Accessed 4 Sep, 2018. https://www.blueletterbible.org//lang/lexicon/lexicon.cfm?Strongs=G3056&t=NASB

4 "G5143–trechō–Strong's Greek Lexicon (NASB)." Blue Letter Bible. Accessed 28 Sep, 2018. https://www.blueletterbible.org//lang/Lexicon/Lexicon.cfm?Strongs=G5143&t=NASB

5 "Commission." Merriam-Webster.com. Accessed September 4, 2018. https://www.merriam-webster.com/dictionary/commission.

6 Excerpt From: Mark T. Barclay. *How to Relate to Your Pastor*. iBooks. https://itunes.apple.com/us/book/how-to-relate-to-your-pastor/id576874638?mt=11

7 https://www.brainyquote.com/quotes/abraham_lincoln_143183

Chapter Three

8 "G4190–ponēros–Strong's Greek Lexicon (NASB)." Blue Letter Bible. Accessed 28 Sep, 2018. https://www.blueletterbible.org//lang/Lexicon/Lexicon.cfm?Strongs=G4190&t=NASB

9 David Jeremiah, *My Heart's Desire: Living Every Moment in the Wonder of Worship* (Nashville: Integrity Publishers, 2002), 63.

10 "H6175–ʿaruwm–Strong's Hebrew Lexicon (NASB)." Blue Letter Bible. Accessed 9 Oct, 2018. https://www.blueletterbible.org//lang/Lexicon/Lexicon.cfm?Strongs=H6175&t=NASB

11 "H6484–patsar–Strong's Hebrew Lexicon (NASB)." Blue Letter Bible. Accessed 9 Oct, 2018. https://www.blueletterbible.org//lang/Lexicon/Lexicon.cfm?Strongs=H6484&t=NASB

Chapter Four

12 "G3056–logos–Strong's Greek Lexicon (NIV)." Blue Letter Bible. Accessed 13 Nov, 2018. https://www.blueletterbible.org//lang/lexicon/lexicon.cfm?Strongs=G3056&t=NIV

13 "G1754–energeō–Strong's Greek Lexicon (NASB)." Blue Letter Bible. Accessed 27 Nov, 2018. https://www.blueletterbible.org//lang/Lexicon/Lexicon.cfm?Strongs=G1754&t=NASB

14 "G2784–kēryssō–Strong's Greek Lexicon (NASB)." Blue Letter Bible. Accessed 27 Nov, 2018. https://www.blueletterbible.org//lang/Lexicon/Lexicon.cfm?Strongs=G2784&t=NASB

Chapter Five

15 Exodus 17:12, "But Moses' hands were heavy. Then they took a stone and put it under him, and he sat on it; and Aaron and Hur supported his hands, one on one side and one on the other. Thus, his hands were steady until the sun set."

Chapter Six

16 http://www.oprah.com/relationships/Negat...

17 "G5318–phaneros–Strong's Greek Lexicon (NASB)." Blue Letter Bible. Accessed 30 Nov, 2018. https://www.blueletterbible.org//lang/lexicon/lexicon.cfm?Strongs=G5318&t=NASB

18 *Theological Wordbook of the Old Testament,* Olive Tree version, R. Laird Harris, Editor Gleason L. Archer, Jr., Associate Editor Bruce K. Waltke, Associate Editor (c) 1980 by The Moody Bible Institute of Chicago, 194 בָּאַר (bāaar) declare, make plain.

19 https://www.merriam-webster.com/dictionary/communicator

Chapter Seven

20 "H8176–sha`ar–Strong's Hebrew Lexicon (NKJV)." Blue Letter Bible. Accessed 1 Jan, 2019. https://www.blueletterbible.org//lang/lexicon/lexicon.cfm?Strongs=H8176&t=NKJV

21 Proverbs 4:23, "Above all else, guard your heart, for everything you do flows from it" (NIV).

22 "G3049–logizomai–Strong's Greek Lexicon (NASB)." Blue Letter Bible. Accessed 4 Jan, 2019. https://www.blueletterbible.org//lang/Lexicon/Lexicon.cfm?Strongs=G3049&t=NASB

23 Matt 21:18-19, "Now in the morning, when He was returning to the city, He became hungry. Seeing a lone fig tree by the road, He came to it and found nothing on it except leaves only; and He said to it, 'No longer shall there ever be any fruit from you.' And at once the fig tree withered."

24 Isaiah 6:3, "And one called out to another and said, 'Holy, Holy, Holy, is the Lord of hosts, the whole earth is full of His glory.'"

25 "G4375–prosphilēs–Strong's Greek Lexicon (NASB)." Blue Letter Bible. Accessed 4 Jan, 2019. https://www.blueletterbible.org//lang/Lexicon/Lexicon.cfm?Strongs=G4375&t=NASB

26 https://www.brainyquote.com/topics/morality

Chapter Eight

27 John C. Maxwell Quotes. BrainyQuote.com, BrainyMedia Inc, 2019. https://www.brainyquote.com/quotes/john_c_maxwell_380196, accessed January 21, 2019.

28 American Heritage® Dictionary of the English Language, Fifth Edition. S.v. "wisdom." Retrieved January 21 2019 from https://www.thefreedictionary.com/wisdom

29 "H2451–chokmah–Strong's Hebrew Lexicon (NASB)." Blue Letter Bible. Web. 14 Apr, 2020. <https://www.blueletterbible.org//lang/lexicon/lexicon.cfm?Strongs=H2451&t=NASB>.

30 Gleason L. Archer Jr.; Robert Harris; Bruce K. Waltke, *Theological Wordbook of the Old Testament*, Chicago, Moody, 1980

31 "H6098–'etsah–Strong's Hebrew Lexicon (NASB)." Blue Letter Bible. Accessed 12 Feb, 2019. https://www.blueletterbible.org//lang/Lexicon/Lexicon.cfm?Strongs=H6098&t=NASB

32 "H1369–gĕbuwrah–Strong's Hebrew Lexicon (NASB)." Blue Letter Bible. Accessed 13 Feb, 2019. https://www.blueletterbible.org//lang/Lexicon/Lexicon.cfm?Strongs=H1369&t=NASB

33 1 Chronicles 11:10, "Now these are the heads of the mighty men whom David had, who gave him strong support in his kingdom, together with all Israel, to make him king, according to the word of the Lord concerning Israel."

34 Luffman, William. *Disgraceful Grace: How the Wonderful Gift of God's Grace Has Been Misrepresented and Abused*. N.p.: William Luffman Ministries, 2018.

35 Piccola, Bob Piccola. *The Key of David*. Apple Books. https://itunes.apple.com/us/book/the-key-of-david/id1236930485?mt=11

www.ingramcontent.com/pod-product-compliance
Ingram Content Group UK Ltd.
Pitfield, Milton Keynes, MK11 3LW, UK
UKHW022220230426
12048UKWH00016BA/963